LEADERSHIP YOURSELF!

Leadership Lessons
From an Air Force OTS Instructor

TYLER WARREN

ISBN:
ISBN-13: 978-1517397272
ISBN-10: 1517397278

Dedicated to Rickey Anderson

My supervisor, my peer, my friend, my accomplice, and my one-stop shop for inspirational motivation.

Special thanks to my wife, Andrea, to all my children, to each of the many instructors who inspire me, to my former Commander Shannon Juby, and to my little sister Katelyn.

CONTENTS

INTRODUCTION

I recently concluded my dream assignment as an Officer Training School (OTS) instructor. OTS is the Air Force's premiere leadership school for new officer accessions. Aspiring officers come to OTS to be trained and indoctrinated in the basics of Air Force leadership; think of it as the "boot camp" for new officers. Think of me as one of those friendly, yet firm, "drill instructors," but focused on leadership development, not just immediate compliance to orders.

I spent three years instructing and training a diverse set of men and women who had in common a love of country and a desire to improve themselves.

On a professional level, I loved my experience as an instructor more than any other work I've done. The lessons I learned while teaching and practicing leadership were immeasurable.

The purpose of this book is to share with you some of the leadership lessons I gleaned during the process of training thousands of new Air Force officers.

I've been encouraged by numerous students, fellow instructors, and Commanders to write this book. What you're about to read is the result of that encouragement.

My target audience is new officers and leaders; those beginning their journey into the world of ever increasing responsibility.

This book was written because there are a few things I'd like you to understand as you start making decisions that will have serious, long-lasting impacts.

My hope for you is that you jump into your first assignment and organization with soberness, ready and able to *leadership yourself.*

Tyler Warren

LESSON ONE

Leadership is art.
You are the artist.
You have the vision.
The canvas is people.
The medium is motivation.
And the gallery in which it hangs, is life itself.

Leadership is art.

Let's start with the end first; where I ended as an instructor of leadership. Three years, a dozen full classes, a thousand faces, and the story of human growth played out, over and over again right before my eyes. It never got old, but it kept getting better.

In preparation for what I felt would be one of my last auditorium lectures, I sat down at my desk and once again asked the question, "what is leadership?" A question I used to hate, but sitting at my desk pondering it yet again, reflecting on all I'd seen, done, and taught, the answer was simple; one word; leadership is...art.

It's something we imagine, visualize, and construct through great struggle and when complete we stand back and admire it. To help the mind grasp what I mean by "art," let me expound on it a little. Art has elements, a medium, an audience, a creator, a motivation, etc. If leadership is art and it has those elements, what are they?

You are the artist. You have the vision.

The artist is you, the leader. The leader approaches the canvas and has the joy and responsibility of making something beautiful happen. The artist has the vision, has the outcome in mind before starting. The artist sees the end from the beginning and goes to work to give it shape and life.

The canvas always starts out plain, empty, white, open; the symbol of both nothingness and limitless possibility. That blank nothingness can become anything, but it is dependent on the vision of the artist. Every visual artwork I've ever created shares one thing in common, they began the same, as nothing but a vision in my mind of what might be.

The leader, you, must have the vision. The creative process behind the artwork we see all around us doesn't start with activity, but begins with thinking, pondering, imagining, sitting quietly, and inquisitively gathering the vision of what should be. Once that image is clear in your mind, it's time to step up to the canvas and act.

The canvas is people.

To those who paint the canvas is a stretched white cloth, or compressed paper, or gesso covered board, for musicians the canvas is the sound of silence, for sculptors the canvas is clay or stone, but for leaders, the canvas is people--their conduct and character.

Art is judged by what is left behind on the canvas. We could judge Michelangelo or Leonardo by the paintings, sculptures, and scientific thought they left for us, but to measure a leader we look at the character of the others they produce. The true measure of leadership are the markings left on the canvas of people.

The medium is motivation.

The leadership medium isn't acrylics, or red clay, or the vibration of strings through the air, or the concussion of drums, but motivation--the will to act.

Your leadership pursuit is a quest to become the master of human motivation. You shape the future based on the activities of subordinates, peers, and partners. Motivation is a complex medium, never quite the same from one person to the other. Some are motivated by a desire to achieve, others by duty, or money, and others still by their personal goals and aspirations.

The leader is succeeding when they begin to see their own motivations reflected back to them in the activities of others, when the canvas begins to reflect the vision of the leader.

The gallery in which it hangs is life itself.

When artwork is finally completed, the artist places it somewhere for observation, contemplation and enjoyment; a museum, a park, a concert hall, or other institution. The gallery that displays the artwork of leadership is *life itself.*

As human beings we have a natural love of leadership; we revel in it, we write homages to historic examples, and we perpetuate leadership philosophies long after the leaders themselves are forgotten. Great leadership is, itself, often more revered than the personalities that produced it. We reflect on it, we ponder it, we are inspired by it, we live by it, because above all else, leadership is the ultimate human art.

Reflect for a moment on all you are, or desire to be. Where did that come from? If you're honest with yourself and set aside selfish pride for a minute, you'll discover that most of what makes you the way you are, was the result of someone else's good or poor leadership. A parent, a boss, a teammate, a friend, a lover, a coach, etc.

Even your desire to be a leader was likely the result of someone developing you, placing trust in you, mentoring you, grooming you, and helping you grow.

Their vision of what you could become is now reflected in your own actions. Your life, all life, is the gallery; the immutable and constant display of countless ages of practiced leadership.

Each new OTS class brought us about 100 - 320 new artists, of different skill levels, ready to further develop their talents in the art of leadership.

The only thing I've found more rewarding than creating art, is creating artists, and that is exactly what I tried to do for each of my students.

Leadership is art. You are the artist. You have the vision. The canvas is people. The medium is motivation. And the gallery in which it hangs, is life itself.

LESSON TWO

Leadership is perhaps best understood when called by its other name--Ownership!

Now let's go back to the beginning, back to the start of my assignment as an instructor.

When I arrived at OTS I was in the process of completing my Masters Degree in Innovative Leadership. The professor in each of these leadership classes would inevitably ask the same question, "What is *your* definition of leadership?"

I hated this question. I mean *really* hated this question. Many students would immediately fire off clever one-liners from one famous source or another. As for me, I was always stumped. I wanted to answer, but just couldn't find the words.

My own experiences in various leadership roles only made it more difficult to answer, because leadership had so many different expressions and caveats.

I would think to myself, "How can you put leadership and its thousand dimensions into a concise thought that doesn't inadvertently leave something out? Any definition just demonstrates its own limitations. Leadership is so much more than a clever sentence-long limerick!"

It also felt wrong to simply quote someone else's definition for leadership; it seemed to imply I hadn't come to any conclusions on my own.

But I admittedly couldn't answer the question to my own satisfaction and could never put forth an answer to those professors. So the question persisted, always nagging somewhere in the back of my mind, "what *is* leadership, really?"

This was my dilemma as I arrived at OTS. I quickly realized I needed to have *my* answer to that very question; with conviction, and articulated in a way that every student would comprehend it.

I was not about to put myself in the awkward position of standing in front of a group of new military officers with my mouth open and nothing to say. Heaven forbid a student should ever ask, "Sir, what is *your* definition of leadership?" and I stand there with the figurative microphone in hand muttering only "uhhhhhh, I'll get back to you."

So, as all artists do, I sat down (amid the shouts of fellow instructors and new cadets), to write the answer. I reflected for several hours on my time in the Marine Corps, my experiences as a father of then six children, my many responsible church positions, my many mentors and examples, and my time spent writing speeches for General Officers. I settled on something basic, a single word: *ownership*.

Effective leaders take ownership of their projects and associate their own identity with the outcomes. Quite often owners even stamp their family name on what they lead (McDonald's, Kohl's, Sony, Kohler, Abercrombie & Fitch, Cadbury, etc. etc.) To think as the owner, I reasoned, could produce only one result, enthusiastic leadership.

On my Flight Commander welcome slides I placed a large blue banner that read, as shown in the title of this section, "Leadership is best understood when called by its other name--Ownership." Finally I had my answer to the question, "what is leadership?"

The question that had plagued me for years was now something I could explain to my students with one simple, but powerful word: ownership.

Through process of time, the word became the basis for the analogy, which took visual form, drawn out on white boards in front of sixteen students, then conference rooms seating fifty, and eventually presented by projector in an auditorium with over four hundred. Now, I want to share it with you.

Let's start with something simple (prepare to have your mind blown).

What is this?

A square...

I know right, mind blown!

Not much yet, but let's draw it out a little bit more.

Now what is it?

> Maybe a building, maybe a home or business, some kind of structure, a garage...

Let's add some hamburger stickers in the windows, some benches, a clown sitting out front that you can take your picture with, and a big M on the top, etc.

Now what do we have?

McDonald's?

For the sake of the analogy, it's a fast food place, perhaps a McDonald's, but this could be many other organizations really and it would work the same.

Now let's add someone to this picture

Who is this?

He's young, has a name tag, a headset, a big smile, enthusiasm for life, a hamburger in one hand, and a spatula in the other.

> The server, the cook, me, the waiter, a worker, a high schooler, my little brother...

You're getting there, this guy is the <u>employee</u>.

So what does an *employee* think about? If you've ever been a McDonald's (or other fast food) employee, what did you think about? Or, if you can't relate to fast food, then think of any entry level, low skill, hourly-wage job and reflect for a minute on what occupied your thoughts as that employee.

> This sucks. How long do I have to be here? Where's my money? Can I get a discount on Fillet-o-Fish? My boss is a jerk. Ugh, not another bus rush! Is this really all I want to do with my life? I wonder what my girlfriend is up to. I wish I had a Mustang convertible...etc.

While working, a typical employee is most often thinking about *not* working. Their focus is on themselves, their own interests, their own needs and wants and meeting the minimum requirements of the job. The job is a vehicle for them to do *other* things.

Now let's draw another character.

Who is this?

He's older, a little thinning on top, a more serious demeanor, wears a nice shirt and tie, carries a briefcase and presents an overall professional image.

> The dad, the doctor, the health inspector, my grandpa, the boss, the manager...

Getting close, but yes, this is the <u>owner</u>.

So what does an *owner* think about?

Money, (in more real terms like income, expenses, liabilities, rent, taxes, cash flow, etc.) customer satisfaction, cleanliness, process throughput, operations, employee welfare, healthcare, local government planning and politics, process improvement, short-term goals and targets, long-term goals and targets, corporate guidance, maintenance, security, accessibility, contracts, health inspections, quality control, competition, marketing and promotion, supply, hiring and firing, training, benefits, laws and statutes, and on and on and on...in a single word, *everything*.

The owner thinks about everything.

Consider what might happen when the French-fry machine breaks down?

What does the employee think?

> "Yes! Don't have to deal with that now, no grease layer on my face tonight. I'll just tell people to go somewhere else for fries."

What does the owner think?

> "This needs to be fixed and fast. Is it under warranty? Do I have a service contract for this? How soon can they be here? How long will it be down? Does it need replacement or maintenance? Who's my supplier? Do I need to get help from corporate? How can I offset customer expectations, should I offer free fries on their next visit? It's been a hard quarter already, I can't lose more customers...etc. etc."

Same issue, very different perspective. The employee might well think "look dude, I just work here...if the things down, it's down, nothing I can do about it."

But the owner, looks at the issue through a different lens. The owner knows that customers will be arriving approximately every minute to trade their money for those tasty fries that he can no longer produce. To the owner it isn't just fries, it's their reputation at stake, and it's their future at stake. It means something deeper.

"Owners" and "Employees" think and act differently.

Owner	Employee
Vision for the future	View of the present
What needs to be done?	What do I need to do?
Purpose and Mission	Tasks
Time invested	Time working or time off
Solutions to problems	Not my problem
Identity linked to success	Identity linked to self
Passion for the product	Motivated by pay
Love for the work	Tolerance of the work
I'm responsible	Yes, he's responsible
This is my life	I just work here
If this fails, I've failed	I'll go work elsewhere

This doesn't mean employees are lazy or overly selfish, it just means it isn't "theirs." The owner, on the other hand, does see it as "theirs," they *own* it. Success or failure, production or stagnation, belongs to them and they sense it daily and act on it.

Now let's change this picture in one way. Let's swap out the big M for a big AF.

Owner   **Employee**

The organization isn't a McDonald's anymore, it's the United State Air Force. You are the newly commissioned officers of this organization; who are you?

Think about your role, your rank, and your position. Who are you?

If you understand the intent of OTS training, you'd see that there is only one answer for you, "I am the owner."

You own the Air Force! You own the responsibility for *everything*. As an officer, you have to think like an owner, act like an owner. The days of "I just work here," are not in your future. Because if you don't own it, who does?

If you don't own the people, the processes, the outcomes, the mission, then who will?

Nobody! Nobody is going to step into your role, nobody will fill the office you have been commissioned to fill. Nobody can, nor should anyone else need to. *You* are the owner.

When things are broken you have the requirement to fix them. When things are not broken, you have the requirement to capture the vision of what could be, look ahead, anticipate change, and plan for it. You are now the one responsible to develop your Airmen, see that they are being taken care of, lead, instructed, guided, mentored and groomed for success.

If the mission is going to be accomplished, the enemy destroyed and defeated, the high standard of professionalism met, or the stage set for victory in the battles to come, it will be because you (and I) make it so. *Everything* is your concern; it's where your day begins and ends.

There will be times ahead when things are hard, problems are complex, pressures are serious, and needs urgent. You might have a tendency to start thinking like an employee;

> "This sucks, why is my Commander such a jerk, why are the days so long, can't I get a break? Another mission! Ugh, why? We're already short. Another deployment, with only three weeks notice, really? I don't want to do this."

On those days, I ask you to reflect back to the silly pictures in this book and remind yourself who *you* are.

You are the owner, not the employee. You are no longer eligible to think like an employee. The Air Force did not hire you to do a job, it commissioned you as an officer. You were given legal and moral authority and obligations that, as long as you serve honorably, cannot be undone. The weight of responsibility for the success of the organization now rests on your shoulders.

Speaking of shoulders, look at them from time to time, what's on them? The rank insignia of an officer, of an official who is expected to act on behalf of the United States, with powers all the way up to and including the ending of human life. That burden of conscience is now inescapably yours.

Leadership is perhaps best understood when called by its other name--Ownership!

Owner   Employee

LESSON THREE

Integrity; Integrity means something is in reality what it appears to be on the outside and when tested, proves to be such.

"Integrity first" is the principle Air Force Core Value. When I would ask my students to define integrity, the response was usually some variation of a quote attributed to General Colin Powell, "Integrity means doing the right thing, even when no one is looking."

I don't disagree with this at all, but I would like to expand on the concept of integrity a little bit by using another representational analogy.

To envision integrity, let's start by thinking of structural integrity. When we look at a building with structural integrity we assume it was built and framed in a way that the walls will bear the weight of the roof, that the foundation is stable and that the building itself can withstand the storms.

When walking into a large auditorium, we assume it has structural integrity. We feel safe. We don't fear the tons of material directly over our heads. We don't imagine it could suddenly come crashing down on us, because the walls have integrity.

Now, imagine sitting in this large auditorium with 300 Air Force officers and picture me walking up to the nearest wall and putting my hand on it. When I push on it, I expect the wall to resist and push back. I expect it to have the structural integrity it needs to bear the weight of the ceiling as well as a little force from my hand.

However, what if someone constructed a wall that looked exactly the same, but built it out of paper instead of steel? It's certainly possible to construct such a facade that outwardly has the appearance of a solid wall. Theme parks and movie sets use false materials all the time.

On the outside it would look the same; it would appear to us to be the same thing, but if I came up to it and as before pressed my hand against the paper wall, instead of pushing back, it would allow me to fall right through it.

These two walls of very different integrity, appeared the same, looked the same, professed outwardly to be the same thing. But when tested, one was true to its appearance and the other was a fake.

So it is with your integrity. Though you declare to have it all day long, though you appear in the same uniform, or with the same demeanor, you only find integrity - or its absence - when it is tested.

And you *will* be tested. Your word will be verified, or nullified by its presence, or absence. Wearing the uniform of the US military and pinning on the rank of officer is your outward declaration of certain standards of conduct and moral character. However, we will not know until you are tested, whether that character is really there or not.

We only find out if you have integrity when we're counting on you, when we need your help, when we need you to execute the responsibilities of the office you hold.

Integrity is integral to officership. In the "Oath of Office." It reads: "I, [your name], do solemnly swear that I will support and defend the Constitution of the United States against all enemies, foreign and domestic; that I will bear true faith and allegiance to the same; that I take this obligation freely, without any mental reservation or purpose of evasion; and that I will well and faithfully discharge the duties of the office upon which I am about to enter. So help me God."

I used to ask my students to tell me where in the Oath of Office is the guarantee that they (or anyone else) will keep the Oath. Where in those few lines is my assurance that you will not violate your word?

Within the Oath there is no prescribed penalty, nor punishment for violators, no statement of physical collateral, or indenture. So what reassurance are you giving me that the Oath will be honored?

Most students struggled with the answer, but a handful over the years surprised me when they responded correctly.

The answer is this: "the *integrity* of the person taking the Oath, *is* the guarantee it will be upheld." The integrity of the men and women raising their hands and declaring their allegiance, is the foundational safeguard of officership.

When I deployed to Central Command Headquarters, I learned an interesting tale of integrity that had compounded the already complex situation in Iraq.

When we agreed to help the Iraqi Army fight against the rising threat from the Islamic State, the question in the backs of many minds was "what happened to their forces? When we left, we had reports of much greater strength and capability then is presently constituted. Where did it go?"

As the military loves to do, we conducted a study. In that study we declared the number one factor hindering the Iraqi forces to be "lack of leadership." What we also found was routine overstatement of forces. I loved to explain this overstatement to my students with a simple exercise.

Imagine we have 10 military units and one Commander for each. The Commanders have overall responsibility for the units, including the distribution of pay.

So I walk down the road with my metal cart full of money and ask the first Commander, "how many in your unit?" He responds, "16." I take from my cart of money enough pay for 16 and hand it to him. "Here's money for 16, make sure everyone gets paid."

I roll my little money cart onto the next Commander and ask the same question, "how many in your unit?" He responds, "15," and I hand him money for 15 and ask him to ensure everyone gets paid.

And so I continue from unit to unit, at some point I pause and encourage the students (who are acting as Commanders) to imagine they lacked a little bit of integrity in their answers. Having already seen that they will get paid based on whatever they report and that no one is checking the validity of the numbers.

Soon the numbers in each unit (which are only actually 16) are inflated to 20, 30, 40, and accordingly I hand them money to pay for their reported strength.

Everyone is smiles and full of giddiness. The lapse in integrity isn't viewed as bad. On the contrary it's kind of fun, it's good, we get more money. All is well. It's only a little lie and it benefits all of us, or so it appears.

I interrupt their rejoicing with an urgent message, "we are under attack!" I tell them we need 100 good men to hold the East line and repel the invasion. I call up their units based on their *reported* strength. With looks of alarm, they stammer and hesitate and the looks of joy turn to fear. The 100 strong they need for victory is only 50 or 60. We fall to the enemy. Everyone dies!

Did it matter? Integrity; did it matter? No. Not when we were receiving the extra money for forces that didn't exist. It didn't matter at all, we were happy, nothing was threating us, nor testing us.

When did integrity matter? Only when it was tested. Only when it was needed. Only when we required the use of the reported forces. Only when we arrived at the battlefront unprepared and scared.

Integrity doesn't matter, all the way up to the point when it *really* matters; not until the real test is upon us and we are forced to face reality with reality; no illusions, no trickery, no lies, and no façade.

When the tests came for Iraq, they were found wanting against a very real enemy, having overstated their forces as much as 20 to 30 percent. It didn't matter; until their nation was crumbling under the weight of a tangible adversary pressing against a mock military force. When it mattered, it was missing.

For you, integrity matters now. It matters always.

And so I say to you, leader: Have integrity, be what you say you are, do what you say you'll do, and when the challenges come, bear the weight, withstand the trials and hold fast to what is right. You are now a projection of your country and military. When the tests come, and they will come, I need you to be in reality what you project to the world to be; the best military force in history. It matters, because in the Air Force, above all else, integrity is first.

Integrity means that something is in reality what it appears to be on the outside and when tested, proves to be such.

LESSON FOUR

Never Arrive.

It took me almost two years and more than 10 classes to finally discover *why* I wanted to be an instructor. The flight I was training at the time called themselves the "Bravo Bunch," and no matter how hard they tried to please me, I always feigned disappointment. They had a test average of 95% and my feedback was, "it should have been 100." Every week of training they were either number one in the class (of 21 flights) or somewhere close to it. Their marching was sharp, but the best I would say is "I'm *almost* proud of you; almost." I was a terrible tease, especially once I saw how much they wanted my praise.

Why? Because I had learned from the previous nine classes, that as soon as I offer my approval and praise, the flight quits trying, they stop progressing and in some cases digress. I didn't want to see them stop short of their potential. What they taught me, was that my true intent as an OTS instructor was to produce a generation of officers that *never arrive.*

Picture this, what happens when you arrive at your home after a long road trip?

You pull in the driveway, stop the car, put it in park, shut off the engine, get out, stretch your legs, hug your mom and walk inside, closing the front door behind you. You have arrived.

The thought of getting back in the car and continuing to drive is unthinkable. You have arrived. You're done. The trip, the task, the mission is over and you put no more thought, or energy, or effort into your travels.

When it comes to officers and their journey of leadership, improvement, Command, and decisiveness, that arrival point should never be reached. Goals are good things, have them, but if you have a grand crowning-achievement type goal or lifelong aspiration, know this, once achieved, you will be left with very little motivation, because you will have arrived at the place you set out to be; you'll stop.

For some of my students, just getting to OTS was an arrival point and they were very difficult to train, because in their minds they had already achieved what they had set out to accomplish. That was enough for them. They had made it.

The idea of needing to meet and prepare for further challenges was sometimes upsetting to these students. In some cases the journey that brought them to training was years long. Once they had arrived in that seat in my class, they felt the journey was complete.

As one example, I counseled a certain student near the end of the course. He had failed his initial physical fitness test and was a few days away from taking his final test. He related to me that he would "do his best," which my experience had taught me was really code for, "I'm planning to fail, Sir, and I'm ok with that."

I tried to talk with him about setting and holding the standard, meeting Air Force expectations, and the long-term repercussions of failed fitness tests (discharge being one of them), but none of it mattered to him. All he wanted to tell me about was how long and hard he had worked to get there, about how far he'd come over the last several years, and how he was already very proud of himself. He was ok with failure, because he had arrived, he was done.

Not only did I counsel him, but I brought in my flight Fitness Officer and challenged him to see if he could find ways to motivate the student toward success.

Of course when the fitness test came a few days later, he failed it, as I already knew he would. He arrived; you should not.

Never arrive! Not ever. From the depth of my heart is the plea to every leader; do more! The work of life is always ahead of us, not behind us.

I want you to be great leaders, exemplary leaders, full of character, charisma, and vision. When you become great leaders, you'll continue to inspire actions in others, long after you're gone. Regardless of your level of achievement now, I plead with you to keep going. That's what the "Bravo Bunch" finally helped me see, my own designs and desire as an instructor was to fuel a fire in the hearts of new officers that would never die.

Decide now that you'll continue your journey, expand your horizons, fly on, fly over, fly further. This life will end on its own soon enough; happy is the man still relentlessly striving upward when it does.

Never Arrive.

LESSON FIVE

Don't standardize stupid.

Starting day one of training, we tell new students that they will be standardized at all times; and for good reason. Within most military units standardization is life saving and critical to mission success. Does everyone have a uniform, helmet, weapon, the correct body armor, the right amount of ammunition, a medical kit, etc. Military units rely heavily on standards to ensure readiness and preparedness.

What inevitably happened in the training environment was the principle itself was soon viewed as more important than the outcome it was intended to produce.

It came in many forms, such as an entire class standing in formation in the heavy rain while their water-proof ponchos hung neatly in perfect rows in the classroom, or inversely, an entire class carrying ponchos with them everywhere on campus, even during sunny, cloud free days.

It was sometimes demonstrated by whole flights arriving to their place of duty with no rank insignia on, because one of them had forgotten theirs.

When questioned, the rationale was always the same, "Sir, you told us we needed to be standardized at all times." To which I would respond, "We don't standardize stupid; we standardize excellence; and then we manage the exception."

Using the example of the student with missing rank, we went from one person out of uniform to all sixteen out of uniform. We had standardized the deficiency in the group, not the strength.

If one person can't be in formation because they are not in the right uniform they still had options, they could detail behind the flight, or they could go room to room and ask others if they have a spare rank insignia (they always did), or they could do any of a hundred other things within their power to manage the exception, correct the one, and return the whole group to excellence.

Degradation of the entire unit was never the intent of being standardized, the principle was intended to ensure the opposite, that all were ready and fully equipped, that the best available was distributed to all. However, good principles taken to extremes often became handicaps to success.

In short, your mission is to standardize excellence and manage the exception; *don't standardize stupid.*

LESSON SIX

You don't matter.

What you do matters!

To the Air Force, to the mission, you don't matter. What you do matters. Your actions, your words, your leadership matter, but you do not.

If I have learned anything from watching dozens of retirements and other transitions out of military service, it's that the organization will move on without you. When General Hoffman, an intelligent, sharp, and professional leader, retired it was only a couple days before it was as though he'd never been. The position had been filled, and the reigns had passed to another. He didn't matter. You don't matter, but what you *do* when in that position absolutely matters!

Each responsible position, and in particular Command positions, need competent and passionate people to fill them. But none of those positions are designed around the people who hold them. Instead people are given a chance to step into those roles and are given the obligation to magnify it.

Subordinates with problems are not likely coming to see you on a personal level; they are coming to see their leader, the Officer in Charge, or Commander. They don't want you and your personal influence or powers, they want the powers and influence of the office you are sitting in.

You must understand that they will have much higher expectations of the office (and rank) than they have of you. You must be willing to set aside your personal self to lead affectively.

You have to play the part, make the phone calls, sign the memos, enforce the laws, and advocate for the right things to happen for your subordinates, peers, and the unit. Their faith and trust is being placed in you as a professional officer and not in you as a personal friend.

To help visualize this, consider the brilliantly written scene from Dreamworks' animated movie Megamind:

Titan, the movies Superman-like villain, is about to kill off the films female love interest and as the music builds and smoke fills the sky, we hear the voice of a confident Megamind proclaim, "You dare challenge Megamind!?"

To which Titan responds, "This town isn't big enough for two super-villains!"

Megamind's retort informs him in condescending fashion, "Oh, you're a villain, alright! Just not a super one!" Titan quickly questions, "Oh, yeah? What's the difference?"

And with much glorious fanfare, Megamind emerges in lights and glory, loudly declaring, "<u>Presentation!</u>"

And then the climactic fight scene commences. (One of my favorite movies, go watch it.)

This scene is a wonderfully crafted analogy for a simple leadership truth, the difference between a good leader and a truly remarkable leader is presentation.

Presentation matters! In some cases it may be the only thing that matters. You must understand the art of presentation (I also call showmanship). Stepping into your role means stepping into something bigger than yourself and your self-interests.

Showmanship is not acting or pretending. It is deliberate effort in creating and maintaining your conduct, appearance, and demeanor. It includes careful design, planning, and teamwork.

Remember from chapter one, leadership is art and art isn't just crafted beautifully, it's also presented beautifully.

Imagine you were to go see Chris Rock's live comedy show; ask yourself, "Did I come to see and hear Chris Rock, the man, or the show with the same name?"

Chances are, you're not in attendance to see and hear from Chris Rock, but rather you've come to laugh and be entertained by the show "Chris Rock." The show is funnier than the man, better timed, better produced, better everything. It's been polished, perfected, and crafted to the audience. The jokes and routines have been run through dozens of times and critiqued behind the scenes by a talented staff of comedic artists and advisors. The Chris Rock you spend money to go see is a team effort.

It doesn't mean Chris Rock is not the one behind the wheel, but the man who steps on the stage in that role is much different than the person he is on his own time.

He has a whole real life offstage, just like the rest of us, filled with real joys, sadness, problems, friends, family, aspirations, disappointments, and so on. We don't come to see that Chris Rock, further we don't want to see that Chris Rock, because presentation matters.

My students at OTS did not get, nor did they want, Tyler Warren as their Flight Commander, because Tyler is way too nice, way too accommodating, way too shy, introverted, and too informal to do the job well. It would have been a disaster for *Tyler* to teach officership at OTS.

"Captain Warren" on the other hand is a phenomenal instructor, a model Airman, always energized, always has the right answer, sees everything, and demands the absolute best from everyone.

Captain Warren turned every situation into an analogy of Air Force leadership. Captain Warren held an extremely high standard and ensured students held an extremely high standard. Captain Warren was a carefully crafted and well-practiced presentation of excellence.

Captain Warren had a team of advisers, counselors, trainers, coaches, evaluators, and mentors. Captain Warren, in all his excellence, was the result of thousands of hours of practice, refinement, feedback, and presentation.

In fulfilling the role of Flight Commander, Captain Warren was not fake, but I understood that the position required actions and activities that of my personal self I might never pursue.

I am Tyler Warren and I am Captain Warren, but a large part of Captain Warren is showmanship. Captain Warren is a position, a role, an office. Captain Warren is one of the many roles I have. I am also a father, husband, son, friend, counselor, etc.

For good reason, we do not act toward our children the way we act toward our parents; or teachers, or bosses, or subordinates, or peers, etc.

Each of the roles we play have different bounds, expectations, and purposes. The role of officer is a role different from the others you may have had, and you must learn that role, be the one with the answers, the one with the power, the one who makes decisions, takes action, and leads using good moral judgement.

You need to be polished, smart, practiced, and professional. You need to use your team. You need to get feedback from peers and mentors to learn the role as you continue to practice the art of leadership.

In the end, you won't matter, but what you've done will matter. What you've done will be remembered.

You don't matter. What you do matters!

LESSON SEVEN

Never listen to critics...
unless they know something, then listen carefully.

All of us know how easy it is to be a critic. Just think back to the last movie you watched; suddenly you turn into a cinema expert and explain all the ways in which the movie should have been better, or could have been worse; in writing, directing, acting, casting, costumes, etc.

Having never attempted the art of making a movie yourself, you offer up vocal (or blogged) criticism to the hundreds of people who just spent the last several years creating that movie.

But does your critical take (no matter how articulate or humorous) matter?

Not really. Would you expect the director or studio to then sit down with you and capture your brilliant ideas about their movie making ability, so they could make changes in the future? Of course not.

But if you were Steven Spielberg, or John Lasseter, then likely that studio or director may show some greater interest in your opinions. Why? Because they have extensive experience and knowledge about the work. Those who create art invariably learn that some critics matter, and most do not. As a leader you will create art, and your art will have many critics.

Back in 2010, Steve Jobs had some email exchanges in response to Gawker blogger Ryan Tate's criticism of the recently launched iPad. Jobs concluded the debate with, "By the way, what have you done that's so great? Do you create anything, or just criticize others work and belittle their motivations?"

Polite or not, the message is poignant--what value does your criticism have to me? Do you know what it takes to imagine, prototype, produce, and market a billion dollar product? Or do you just observe, consume, and comment about perceived faults?

My experiences working closely with several Generals, has taught me, among other things, that they operated under the constant pressure of critics. At the senior levels these critics included media, Congress, US citizens, and even the President. A single decision could be hailed by some and booed by others.

I witnessed willful media misreporting of events, whose details I was privy to because of my position. I saw undo criticism from citizens and academics who had no experience or wisdom about the complexity of running massive military operations. I saw uninformed criticism of military actions taken by soldiers under indescribable stress and fear, but judged harshly by those who've never felt such fear, nor likely ever will.

You will have many critics. Some will laud you as the best, some will point to your faults and some will simply comment on your leadership with indifference. Some critics will compliment you in person, while they grumble about you to their friends. Only a small portion of these critics should matter to you.

Be very weary of critics (even if senior in rank) who have no real relevant experience. But pay close attention to those who have lived and learned, who have insights, who are also creators and builders, and who know what it takes to be successful.

OTS was also full of critics. As a matter of policy, The Air Force loves feedback and every student had the right and obligation to provide their input on the course objectives.

This feedback was then religiously reviewed by instructors, supervisors, Commanders, and even the Commandant.

Some of the feedback students offered us was genuinely helpful or full of praise for the course. Most was complaints, and criticism, while a small portion was just crazy town (I mean really crazy town).

Almost all of us as new instructors took student criticism extremely hard. The level of passion and commitment needed to be an instructor, combined with the endless hours required, made us especially hungry for praise. We wanted to feel that our hard work mattered to these newly trained officers.

To have a student turn around and offer mean spirited jabs could hurt a lot. Well, at least initially. After a few rounds I came to understand that almost all of them had no idea what it takes, behind the scenes, to put together and execute a production as big as OTS. They couldn't see it for what it was. They could only see through the lens of themselves (like the person watching the movie, or the mid-20s news reporter commenting on combat).

The pain of undue criticism taught me an important, but hidden truth: the students are not the customer of OTS, they are the product.

When I regarded them as customers, I took actions to adjust my behavior to accommodate their comfort and perceptions. But no matter how much we adjusted to them, it was never enough. They were never satisfied.

Eventually I understood the purpose of the training and realized that the customer of OTS wasn't the students. The customer was really the Air Force; their future units, their future Commanders, their Country. I needed to answer to those units, Commanders, and Country for my actions. Was I doing enough for them? Was I training the students well enough to ensure they would meet the needs of the broader organization?

The inspired mission of OTS, as reimagined by Colonel Scott Lockwood, is "To produce leaders of moral character." The implied context adds "...for the United States of America."

My oft used retort to unjustified student criticism was simple, "You are not the *customer* here, you are the *product.*"

We answer to America, not you. You may not like the training, because it's designed to change you, stretch you, challenge you, and make you better; but know this, we aren't doing it *for* you, we're doing it *to* you. You are the product here. The customer, America, is hungry for more leaders who are selfless, dedicated, honest, consistent, faithful, vigilant, fearless, and just plain good. That's what we are trying to make you into.

The critics I learned to carefully listen to were experienced instructors, course directors, and Commanders. They knew what it took, and I wanted to know better, so I asked, listened, and learned.

I am open to criticism, in fact I seek it! But the sign on the door reads, "members only."

Never listen to critics...unless they know something, then listen carefully.

LESSON EIGHT

Don't tell people what you want them to do.

Tell people what you want done.

Let's start with a story. I had an important package that I needed to send to a friend a few thousand miles away by the next day. I walked into the shipping store and as I paid the service rep an enormous amount of money, the thought occurred to me; what I'm asking them to do is truly unbelievable.

In exchange for a relatively few dollars, I was expecting them to take this box from my location, and transport it across the country and with precision place it safety at the correct house before the end of the next day.

By itself, that's not a simple task. But they not only have my item to transport, but tens of thousands of other packages also trying to get somewhere by the next day. Consider what that network looks like, the gates, rails, planes, trucks, people, and computers that all need to work together in unity of effort to take a nearly innumerable number of parcels and move them around the world with multiple deadlines from hours to days; all as efficiently as possible.

I imagined my box getting handed to someone, scanned, placed on a truck and moved to a bigger regional center, scanned, placed on another truck, scanned, placed on a plane, scanned, flown to a regional center across the country, scanned, placed on another truck, scanned, etc. etc. until it arrives at its destination the next day. This one package of mine would travel by foot, road, air, conveyer belt, etc.

How foolish it would be for me to dictate in any way *how* they intended to get it there. Even if I could see their entire network of connections, I would be entirely out of line to go into further detail about which truck I think it should go on, or what flight it should catch, or which delivery guy should handle it. Doing so would only make the process less efficient and likely would result in the package arriving late.

I needed only tell them what I wanted done, leaving the how to do it to them. And so it is with leading.

Tell your subordinates what you want done and let them figure out how to do it. We often inject inefficiency by wanting to know too much about, or even dictate the way something is done.

I discovered over and over again with my cadets that the more involved I was in the solution process, the less effective the results.

Early on I felt like I was "helping" the students by doing certain tasks for them. What ended up happening was I caused more frustration, time-jacked myself, and prevented them from knowing the details of what was going on.

At one point, I was the staff member responsible for class logistics, which covered the dorms, supplies and food that each trainee would need. To assist me I had a rep from each flight at my command. I learned that telling them the results I wanted, "everyone needs to eat tomorrow morning, it's on you, so figure it out," actually enabled them to manage the solution, adjust to unexpected circumstances, organize themselves, be creative, and accomplish the mission.

I honestly didn't care how food got to everyone, or what food it was, just that everyone got fed. Of course I'd give them the tools to succeed by telling them when the dining hall would be open and what contacts they could call, but beyond that, I left it to them. I learned to never solve the puzzles for them.

When I told students what end-state I needed, it nearly always got done right. When I told them what to do, they nearly always disappointed.

Don't tell people what you want them to do. Tell people what you want done.

LESSON NINE

Rumors are such enjoyable lies.

Go and see for yourself.

As instructors we called it the "student rumor mill," and we were always keenly aware of the stories going around it. This was the channel of useful (often humorous) information. Unfortunately it often entailed false reports of rampant health issues, criminal activity, misuse of position, and evil instructors.

Within the crowd, the telephone game makes rumor and anecdote become common fact, and quickly. Some of these facts, if accurate may require serious corrective action. To illustrate, I'll share just a few stories of rumors and their eventual resolutions.

While acting as the staff officer for safety, I had a serious report come to me through the student safety officer network. The mats being used during daily exercises were spreading staff infections!

Not only did several safety officers report this to me, so did several concerned instructors, worried that we had some epidemic on our hands.

This wasn't my first rodeo. I wasn't worried, not even a little bit. If true, this *would* be a big deal with implications for the program, the OTS campus, the suppliers, etc. If not, it would be another example of the student rumor machine making life interesting.

I gave my student safety officer a simple assignment. "Find me one."

I told him to go from flight to flight (all 21 of them at the time) and collect the names of every student who gone to medical and been diagnosed with staff. Alternately, tell anyone who felt they were infected to report to medical for an exam and bring me their names.

The next day, the report came back, "none, Sir." I responded "You went to every flight room, asked every student, and no one claimed an issue?"

"Yes Sir."

Zero infections, zero students that went to medical for treatment; just a dramatic story.

I took a couple minutes to mentor my safety officer on the topic of misinformation through rumor and of the crucial need to verify the things we hear; to go and see.

I mentioned this wasn't my first Rodeo, and it's hard to even put a finger on which rumor was my first, but some examples prior to this that taught me to be cautious of so-called common knowledge were:

Urgent report from my senior instructors that, "half the class had their uniform tailoring messed up," the day before pictures were to be taken. The result of an exhaustive search...just two had serious issues, and they were able to be resolved the next day.

One cold, windy, and rainy morning a student was feeling ill and dropped out of our exercise session. The student rumor mill promptly reported back a case hypothermia and hospitalization, blaming negligent staff for the casualty. None of which was true.

My favorite, was from my "Bravo Barracudas" (...you know who you are). The report came to me after a seemingly quiet weekend that members of my flight had violated curfew (worthy of a verbal counseling), driven a car while intoxicated (worthy of further disciplinary action and possible disenrollment from the course) and had the military police called to the dorms to arrest them (worthy of serious action and investigation).

We began calling in the students involved and questioned them. The facts of the story were not nearly as interesting as the rumored account. As it turned out, military police had been to the dorms, but in a totally unrelated capacity. The students had been out drinking, but had followed the rules and arranged for a designated driver returning safely. The students had signed in to quarters on time, but after entering the building a few had gone back outside, giving the appearance of being a separate group.

Our findings were that two of the students drank too much alcohol and had behaved inappropriately, but nothing warranting formal disciplinary actions. They were counseled and even presented a 15 minute lecture to the rest of the students about professionalism, and by some measures that was an excessive punishment.

Rumors are fun. They dress up like nuggets of secret wisdom and dramatic insight, but when disrobed, they are just smoke and old sausage, nothing to them, nothing useful. I don't know what in human nature attracts us to rumors, but they are everywhere. An unfortunate reality you will face as an officer, is the need to address them. So I remind you, as I learned too many times:

Rumors are such enjoyable lies. Go and see for yourself.

MORE LESSONS

"Articulation; because brilliant ideas misunderstood are dumb ideas. And dumb ideas well understood too often become fact."

"Making something a little better is not innovation. Building something no one else imagined is innovation. Maybe that's not you, so just make it better anyway."

"Experience teaches what study never can. Love what you learn in your studies, but test it through your experiences. This is knowledge."

"Stop quitting! When I see you quit I can't help but think it's because someone or something in your life has repeatedly taught you that quitting is ok. As long as you did your best, you are successful--as long as it's too hard, as long as you're uncomfortable, just stop and tell yourself you gave your best effort. No mission will ever care if you've given your best, it is either accomplished or failed. You need to stop being willing to fail. Stop quitting."

"[Talking to Lt Bennet:] You know what I see when I look at you, Lieutenant Bennet? I see fire in your eyes... [Turning to the group and shouting] But you need to know something about me Bravo Flight! I'm not a Firefighter...I'm a Pyromaniac! And I want to see that same fire in everyone's eyes!"

"Credibility is the currency of leadership. Credibility is what you need to pay to do whatever you want. If you have it, you can do anything. Credibility is what payed for Jimmy Doolittle's near suicide mission to bomb Tokyo...and credibility is what payed for 80 men to willingly follow him. Credibility is your money."

FINAL LESSON

When all else fails...Leadership Yourself!

When disaster strikes, normalcies fail; economics, infrastructure, law, order, etc. all disappear as the human machine tries to grapple with unexpected change and attempts to grasp onto what *used to be*.

The one thing which emerges as the principle factor between chaos or recovery is leadership.

Leadership is the premiere commodity of the human race. The history of the human family is written in the language of leadership, small and great.

No amount of resources, time, expertise, or other proficiency can compensate for a lack of leadership. Good leadership can accomplish the mission when the only reasonable outcome is failure.

I'll conclude this book in the same way I used to end my auditorium presentations. Understand, this is my heart. Even as I began:

Leadership is art.
You are the artist.
You have the vision.
The canvas is people.
The medium is motivation.
And the gallery in which it hangs, is life itself.

Wars are waged and victories won by leadership.

Air superiority, information superiority, or force superiority, while important, do <u>not</u> provide victory on their own.

Leadership superiority is the only way to guarantee success.

While I was at Central Command, a few hundred Islamic State fighters took and held a city from an Army of twenty thousand; because leadership.

No technology, nor tactic, nor good intent, nor number of soldiers will win against superior leadership.

Make no mistake, my dear friends, we <u>will</u> lose the next conflict in which our enemies bring to the battlefield better leadership than our own!

It has been my mission--the OTS mission--to ensure that cannot and will not happen!

Your future is as bright as your leadership. You have been given all the tools you need to succeed.
Now it is time to,

LEADERSHIP YOURSELF!

The End

OTHER STORIES

"So there I was..."

Being an instructor was a brilliant and fulfilling assignment full of inspiration, character building and human growth.

The work was often quite hard, with 16 and 18 hour days, hot, humid weather, working while sick, and losing your voice, but intermingled with the intense training was some of the most hilarious and unforgettably moments.

It probably helped that by the end of the second week all of us were exhausted, so even little things made us laugh hysterically.

This section is really just for fun, no great lessons to explain, but some stories that were funny at the time. I promise the stories are at least 10% true. If any of these stories aren't particularly humorous to you, well, I guess you just had to have been there.

Guacamole!

As instructors we fed off each other. One brilliant idea in the mind of one instructor became everyone's brilliant idea (and fast). To the students we always seemed fresh and full of clever quips and one-liners that we were perpetually stealing from each other.

Sometimes you'd overhear another's monolog and think, "where on earth are you going with that?"

Captain Chris Wilinski, (one of my favorite instructors and close friend) kicked off a leadership speech to an audience of 50+ students with, "You are all like, Avocados!"

Immediately, those of us listening thought, "what in the world are you going for, Chris?"

And he continued:

> "You start out all green and bumpy, but then we cut you open, tear out the pit and mash you up with some tomatoes, cilantro, onions, salt, and BAM...Guacamole!"

At its heart, the message was good, but the visual left some students with confused looks in their eyes as they pondered how to best become the guacamole we hoped they'd be. Chris later confessed after a lunch at Chipotle, the imagery sounded better in his head than his delivery provided.

Put your pocket in your pants!

Captain Rickey Anderson was the master of the one liner correction. His volume and inflection were spot on. Some of his oft used favorites were "Cup your hands!", "Are you a killer or a clown?", "Hey, Mr. Coffee!", "Get your hands out of your pockets!", and many more.

On one rare occasion he was able to string several of these together (admittedly inadvertently). Marching back to the dorms with my flight, Captain Anderson noticed the flight leader's pocket was inside-out. To make the correction he called out:

> "Hey, flight leader, put your hand in your pocket, then put your pocket in your pants, then get your hand out of your pocket, and cup your hands!"

I know it probably doesn't translate well, but to fellow instructors this was a brilliant exchange, a marvel of serial correction.

Chicken of the Future

Between classes was a wonderful time for us as staff. Instructors would strategize about how we would up the stakes for the next class; things we could do better, the theme of the coming class, what craziness could we expect, what tactics we would use.

We were discussing the name of the Falcon Squadron and what we might describe it as. We brainstormed everything we could think of and eventually out of my mouth came the phrase, "The Falcons are...the chicken of the future!"

The look of bewilderment on the faces of my fellow instructors somehow made it stick. So for that class I referred to the Falcons as the Chicken of the Future.

Strange as it was, so did everyone else, including the students. Which only made it funnier to me.

Near the end of that class the Falcon rep (Captain Segev Phillips) won the class Jeopardy-style "knowledge bowl" by answering the final question with "Chicken of The Future!" Of course it was not the right answer, but he had already out played the other teams and accumulated enough points that it didn't matter. As the answer was read by the moderator, he stood on stage with arms wide open and head leaned back, to the sound of applause from one side and jeers from all the others. The exchange was a highpoint for me.

Twins

Twins could be problematic when they came through the course at the same time. Some looked so alike there was no way to tell which was which. In one particular incident, during the commotion of day one, when the intensity and volume are highest. I was waiting on my flight to complete an assigned task and report to me.

When no one arrived by the set time, I sternly marched from my desk toward the room. I was delayed a little, finding several students needing correction. As I finished talking to the group, I noticed one of my students (Lt Dodge) walking down the hallway.

I called him over, gave him an ear full about tardiness, and for the next couple minutes assigned him a litany of tasks to accomplish. "Lt. Dodge, here's what I need you to do, go back to the room, find Captain so and so, tell him he's late, that this won't be tolerated, also tell him...and...ensure they...and find the group deputy commander...tell her...etc."

83

As I completed my tirade he responded with a funny look on his face, "Sir, I think you have me confused with my twin brother."

At which point I finally looked at his name tag and noticed he wasn't *my* Lt Dodge, he belong to a different flight.

Not to be outdone, and staving off embarrassment, I quickly responded, "Ok, go find your twin brother, tell *him* to do everything I just told *you* to do...and hurry up!"

You're fired!

Each student was assigned at least one and sometimes several leadership positions in the class. We "fired" people from their positions all the time if they failed to meet expectations.

For some students this was the first time in their life they had failed at anything and it brought grown men and women to tears. In all honesty, this was partially the point of the pressure we placed on them, to stress their limits and as a result come to know themselves better.

Emotions and crying aren't funny, but on one occasion Captain Anderson was about to fire his second in

Command for failing to meet deadlines over several days. He called him to his office and was about to deliver the news, but before he could tell him he was fired, the student became emotional and asked, "Sir, I know why you called me here, I know I'm failing...but if you could please step outside for a minute...so I can cry alone, I just...I'm very proud, Sir...and I don't want anyone to see me cry, Sir...please, just for minute."

To his credit, Captain Anderson, not sure what else to do, stepped out and let him cry for a few minutes. When the student was done and put himself back together, Captain Anderson continued, "You okay now? Good, you're fired."

People are stealing stuff

After finishing their meals, the first two members of each flight were expected to march themselves to the front of the building and retrieve their guidon (unit flag on a stick). Early in the program, this was often an easy thing to target for correction.

One memorable instance, I came outside to see my flight without theirs and began to question them.

"Has anyone gone to get the guidon?"

"No, Sir."

"Who is supposed to get the guidon?" No one knew, so they looked it up in their instruction manuals and replied, "Sir, the first two members to come outside."

"Who were the first two out?"

Two responded with, "Sir, we were."

"So who's going to get the guidon?"

"Sir, we are!" And off they went to get it. Not more than 100 yards away they passed right by two other members of the flight with the guidon in tow on their way back from the front of the building, but unfortunately they didn't notice.

Seeing this I could have called them back, but instead I just wanted to observe what they would do if I just let it happen. I expected them to search around for a few minutes than return empty handed when they realized it wasn't there.

About seven minutes go by and I'm about to give up and go get them, when here they come with half a guidon (no flag, and clearly not our staff). As they approach I stop them and ask why they took so long.

They responded matter-of-factly, "Sir, we had trouble finding our guidon, because someone stole the banner off it, but we have the stick."

"Are you *sure* that's ours?"

"Yes, Sir!"

"You're totally sure?"

"Yes, Sir, absolutely sure, this is our stick but the flag was stolen. We suspect it was Alpha Flight playing a prank. Sir, don't worry, we're already working on a plan to take back our flag."

"You mean that flag?" I say pointing to the rest of the flight standing in formation with guidon in hand.

With confidence in their eyes they responded, "Sir, never mind. About Face!" And they turned around and marched the stick back to the front.

I almost lost it laughing (...conceal, don't feel; don't let them know...), but still admired their conviction to their own conclusions. With students, there was never a problem so simple, that they couldn't find a complex solution.

Final, Final Thoughts

Fellow instructors may find those stories humorous, and perhaps those who've been through a basic training experience; for everyone else, I apologize.

I owe a lot to the military. I wouldn't trade my time served for anything. Starting with Marine Corps boot camp, follow on training, and assignments; then as an Airmen, growing through OTS as a student after college; then through many assignments, and time as an instructor, all of which have stretched me, challenged me, and molded me.

So much of the good I possess was discovered and shaped by my military journey. In a positive way, it has changed my perceptions of myself, others, and the world. It allowed me to sit in rooms labeled "Top Secret" that resembled Hollywood movie sets (it's all real by the way) and learn things only few people get to know.

If I can say anything about what I've observed first hand from Commanders at every level and in particular at the highest military ranks, it's that they are some of the best people I've known.

There is a constant sense of seriousness about the work of defending the country. We are incredibly deliberate in our plans and actions.

We are careful, we are calculated, we are as precise as humanly possible, and we are compassionate. Every leader I know, feels the weight of what they are asked to do. Because in addition to being conscientious, there is no escaping the reality that we are lethal.

While I was at Central Command, we (the US military) killed thousands of people. I was awakened to the sobering reality, being privy to the daily war reports, "xx number of targets destroyed last night, xx number estimated casualties."

I can tell you from the sincerity of my heart, it wasn't a joke to any one of us. Everyone felt the burden of it. Everyone took it seriously. Everyone wanted to do the right thing and protect Americans, allies, and the innocent.

I have great confidence in the intelligence and moral character of our military leadership. I've met and worked with the absolute best of men and women. If not so, I wouldn't stick around.

I think the message of the old Marine Corps recruiting poster sums up my final thoughts to you: We're looking for a few good men!

If you *are* good, if you have integrity, if you are among those of high moral courage and if you have a love for your country; <u>you</u> are needed! In one way or another get involved and answer the call to serve. You'll quickly find you're among friends.

Good futures come from good presents. And Good presents are *given* by good people.

About the Author

Tyler Warren is an artist and writer currently serving in the United States Air Force. He first joined the military in 2000 by enlisting in the Marine Corps. He has a BA in Economics and an MA of Innovative Leadership.

Prior to becoming an instructor at Officer Training School, Tyler was the speechwriter to the Commander of Air Force Materiel Command. There he crafted strategic messaging for the 4-star Commander, Vice Commander, and Executive Director. He was honored to have written speeches for the Air Force's first female 4-star, General Janet Wolfenbarger (now retired).

Tyler enthusiastically volunteered for an assignment to Officer Training School where he served as a Flight Commander and Instructor. He directly trained approximately 150 newly commissioned Air Force Officers and presented leadership lessons to several thousand others. While assigned at OTS, Tyler deployed to Headquarters US Central Command.

Tyler earned the prestigious Master Instructor Badge from Air Education and Training Command (AETC); an award given to only the top 5% of AETC instructors.

Tyler and his bride Andrea have eight children and reside in Alabama.

26975502R00056

Made in the USA
Middletown, DE
10 December 2015